Advance Praise for
THE LONG PAUSE AND THE SHORT BREATH

"This collection of poems and photos beautifully illustrates the complex emotions of living in New York during a global pandemic. Nicole's book provides a much-needed sense of comfort. Her words put you at ease, while also reminding us of our humanity and strengthened bond of community we've developed during this pandemic."

~Kelly Ripa, Entrepreneur, Host, Actress and Producer

"As haunting and shattering as it is uplifting. A firsthand account of life in New York City when the virus exploded and culminating in the unrest following George Floyd's murder, all rendered in plain, stripped down language and images that disturb and inspire in equal measure. It's an unrelenting and searing portrayal of a home to millions and cultural mecca brought to its knees. Yet Rubens' lens always manages to find vibrancy in the city on pause, and her genius is illuminating the hope and resilience and redemption in the midst of the anguish."

~ David Grae, Television Writer/Producer *(Madam Secretary, Castle, Gilmore Girls, Without a Trace, Joan of Arcadia)*, Co-Founder Gotham Writers Workshop

"Through the lens of a native New Yorker, an incredible poetic and photographic record of a frightening time, punctuated by positivity. Poems that evoke images and photos that are like poetry. This powerful and poignant book articulates and visualizes the pandemic emotions of the millions of us who live in and love New York. An intimate poetic snapshot of pandemic life in NYC."

~ Jennifer Ratner, Pediatrician, Founder of Friends of the East River Esplanade

Times Square

THE LONG PAUSE
and
THE SHORT BREATH

Poems & Photos - Reflections On New York City's Pandemic

Nicole Freezer Rubens

The Three Tomatoes Book Publishing

Published October 2020
Printed in the United States of America

ISBN: 978-1-7353585-4-3
Library of Congress Control Number: 2020918069

For information address:
The Three Tomatoes Book Publishing
6 Soundview Rd.
Glen Cove, NY 11542

Cover and interior images: Nicole Freezer Rubens
Cover and interior design: Susan Herbst

Shake It Up

Like A Rock

To the exhilarating eternal flame of New York City
that can never be extinguished

Keep This Far Apart

March 25, 2020

Everyone is smiling
during the crisis
and I'm smiling back
and cocking my head
as I walk in Central Park
during the Covid-19
shutdown
lockdown
reset
shelter in place
quarantine
isolation
pause.
Semantics do not matter.
It always killed me
when running or walking
on lakeside paths
in Florida or Connecticut,
when I had to say good morning
to all the strangers in my way.
New Yorkers simply did not do that.
Now, these novel nods and acknowledgements
even from behind a few pale blue masks,
are extraordinary connections.
I love my neighbor
from 6 feet apart
and for a split second,
we are a community.

March 29, 2020

Each morning after I awake
just before the ethereal fog of sleep dissipates,
I remember that Corona is still here.
I set my iPhone alarm
for 6:55 pm
so that at 7
I can exit my apartment
onto my decorative-useless-until-now
Juliette balcony
that adorns the beige brick facade of my building.
I sandwich myself between my neighbors
to cheer for the healthcare workers
who are soldiering on
with Hefty garbage bags for armor.
I can touch my mouth,
stick my pinched thumb and middle finger
under my tongue
and whistle with all my might.
I clap, cheer, whoop and tear,
and at 7:02 I go back
to my orange tufted sofa and iPad
and simply stay there.

Growth

The Morning After

March 30, 2020

Today a field hospital
is being erected in Central Park
on the lawn
where my children's nursery school
had its annual year end family picnics.
These stiff white tarps
draped over life-sustaining poles
serving as pillars of strength,
should be carnival tents.
Masks inside
should be colorful superhero faces,
a Wonder Woman, a Spiderman,
disguising real freckled and dimpled faces
and missing teeth,
yet to know who they will become.
Instead this makeshift medical unit
opens tomorrow for Covid overflow.
68 beds to be filled
by thousands
via the ripple effect each person has.
I can imagine the sound
of the inevitable April showers
as they rain down
on the waterproof canvas.
There is a refrigerated truck,
a long one,
stationed across the street from my house.

It too is accessed
from the rear entrance to the hospital
by way of 2 white tents.
My house is now a fort.
Instead of cannons
braced on my window sill,
I have gallons of hand soap,
canisters of Clorox wipes
and thousand-piece puzzles
to defend my family's
fate and passage of time.
I do not tell my friends about the truck.
There are many sentences that form in my head
but I leave them there,
not to upset anyone further.
If they thought about it
they would know
but there is so much to think about
and too much time to think.
For now my troops feel well
and I am grateful for each hour
when this new normal is as good as this.
I can still walk in my park,
together 6 feet apart from my neighbors,
past the hospital field
where I once laid an old sheet
and ate cold chicken nuggets
dipped in Ketchup,
with my 3 year old.

April 1, 2020

I woke up this morning an April fool
and then remembered
that hundreds of innocent people
will die today.
With all the unpredictability,
this they know.
Yesterday was a down day for me.
I went to the NY Blood Center
to donate whole blood.
Like masks and toilet paper,
there is not enough.
After 2 temperature checks,
typing on a shared computer keyboard
and a finger prick,
I was rejected.
My iron level was a fraction away from viable.
I wanted to do something,
even a small act the size of
a pint of Hàagen-Dazs chocolate ice cream,
to help the cause.
So I went home, washed my hands hard,
and stayed home.
I sat on my couch again and
FaceTimed my mother-in-law
while I ate straight from the pint.

Masks Do Grow On Trees

Up And Down

April 2, 2020

Today I learned
that my friend Lisa's
100 year old grandmother
tested positive.
I immediately sent Lisa
the CNN article about
the 102 year old woman in Italy
who recovered from Corona.
There was a photo of her
with a yellow frosted birthday cake
that was bigger than she used to be.
2 weeks ago
Lisa's grandma got up,
got dressed
and her son took her to McDonald's
for an Egg McMuffin
and a cup of coffee.
She loves their coffee.
He bought her another scratch off
but I don't know what she won that day.
Today she's at New York Cornell
in a lovely room
with a river view
and an oxygen tank.
All hospital rooms are now ICUs.

Her grandson is a doctor there
and he can dress up
from balding head
to rubber shoed toe,
and see her.
This is a luxury.
They think she may not know it's him
beneath the disposable paper suit,
but I think she does.
And in her mind
she's thinking about
her well lived life
and biting into her next Big Mac
while waiting patiently and gracefully
for her coffee to cool.

April 3, 2020

And today I wear a mask
as I venture out
into the epicenter of the storm.
Face coverings have now been mandated.
I walk past the refrigerated truck
and see they have added a second one.
My daughter's aqua bandana
loosely covers my nose and mouth
so no one can see my expression.
My costume could be a cowgirl bandit
or maybe a bank robber
in a cashless society.
It prompts me again
to stay quiet
and not tell my friends.

Objects In The Mirror Are Closer Than They Appear

A Day In The Life At Home

Squeaky Clean

Half Mast

April 4, 2020

It's the start of week 4
in lockdown
and a routine has set in.
This is the most glorious morning yet,
temperate, and the light
is a specific kind of golden.
This is it.
This might be the week of the apex in New York City,
with a new abundance of deaths
that will flatten the curve
and then head downward
toward recovery,
recovery of mutant civilizations,
an immense variation of our old mundane ways.
The American dream program
has been interrupted.
I feel a bit too excited
to collectively jump this hurdle
when it means
800 actual people
might die in 1 day
and the term
temporary internment
may be a necessary reality
inside our beautiful parks,
never meant for this kind of refuge.

I walk past Lasker Rink
which is slowly melting and puddling
over the red and blue ice hockey demarcations.
It will not likely
become a public pool this summer,
as it's meant to be.
It was urban planned
for multipurpose,
like my blue bandana
I now use as a face covering
to avoid spreading Covid
in case I have it
and am lucky enough not to know it.
I can kill someone
by simply stepping outside
without a mask.
We cannot call them masks though,
as the proper PPE
needs to be reserved
for the bravest of our healthcare workers
who are far more than
multipurpose right now.

April 7, 2020

I count to 5
all day long,
constantly measuring,
Lexie,
Julia,
Valerie,
Doug
and me.
I used to do a head count
each morning
but then they moved out,
one by one.
Now again I set the dinner table
each night
with 5 plates,
5 knives,
3 salad forks,
and 2 grown up forks.
The girls still prefer small silverware.
5 glasses,
5 napkins.
If we order in
5 main courses
in my shopping cart,
one no onions,
one no peppers
and there is a gluten free.
For now,
everything is contact free delivery.
I bless the folks
who show up at their jobs
to cook my dinner.
There could not be 6 feet
between chefs
at the blistering hot grill.

They risk their lives to make burritos,
and I risk mine by supporting them.
How long does Corona last
on refried beans?
After dinner the daily death toll
appears on all my screens,
the constant count
of people
who should still be counting
their blessings
and their silverware.
But each and every night
I am graced with this bonus season together,
cloistered at home,
like once again it's 2015,
the last time we all lived under one roof.
This is the silver lining.
This is something that cannot be undone.
This cannot be taken away from us, ever.
We own each puzzle piece,
each text and eye roll.
This is the prize of time.
Some dinners are raucous
and some are routine,
but each and every night of lockdown
we take our forever seats
at the kitchen table
and pass the plastic water pitcher
around 5 times.
Afterwards
I scrub the kitchen extra hard
to keep us safe
for tomorrow's breakfast.

Calgon, Where'd You Go?

Stained

April 8, 2020

Tonight is the first Seder.
I am rarely home for Passover
but almost always in Rochester
with family.
I set the table
with my yellow and blue
wedding registry Monet dishes
and Nana and Pa's
filthy, beaded, silk matzah cover,
with the kind of golden fringe
only found on a ritual object
from a mother country.
My Seder plate
with slightly sunken designated areas
for the Passover symbols,
is from a Jonathan Adler warehouse sale.
Each symbol tells our story
of going from slavery to freedom.
10 plagues liberated us from Egypt
and now a novel plague
keeps all of us down.

Seder means order.
Tonight we will have a Seder
with a computer on the table,
connecting a grid
of nuclear families.
We will be together apart
but united by a big cracker
and some extra bitter herbs.
After we close our laptops
and sweep up the inevitable
matzah crumbs from the floor,
we will go to sleep knowing
that tonight once again,
nothing could stop us.
We were part
of a new kind of celebration
shared by every Jew
and their guests
around the world.

April 12, 2020

A month ago
there were little bombs
dropping every day.
Wash your hands,
Purell,
start to stock up
but do not hoard.
Separate tables at restaurants.
Close schools and universities.
No gyms.
Turn off the spotlights
and darken Broadway stages
and museum walls.
Work from home.
Stay home.
Teach your children well.
Save lives.
Daily detonations
raining down,
destroying our undervalued prosaic strolls
down grocery aisles.

4 weeks in
and now we are drifting
with no new instructions
for us soldiers.
5 star hotels
are now dormitories for doctors
and homeless people
who are still homeless.

My friend Susie
turns 53 today.
A Zoom gathering
was as good as it could get,
but it's so hard to speak
when connected to so many boxes
of blurry faces.
I tend to interrupt people
and I can't.
It's like learning to talk again.
When I meet up virtually
I get distracted
by everyone's backgrounds.
Setting up shop
in front of curated bookshelves
seems quite popular.
And then I remember to
check out how I look
and no one looks good on FaceTime or Zoom.
Trying to be present,
I could see Susie's flourless cake
but I could not enjoy
the smell of
her blown out candle,
which is one of my favorite smells.
Happy Birthday dear Susie,
Happy Birthday to you.

There's A Birthday In The House

A Long Way To Go

April 13, 2020

It's Monday of week 5.
The weather is bad.
Severe rainstorms are ripping through
and threatening
the outdoor tented pop-up hospitals.
60-70 mile per hour winds
are blowing germs
and oxygen lines.
Tornadoes rake the south.
Mississippi and Georgia
lost some people
to a different, non-novel disaster.
Shards of sharp metal
that yesterday were small planes,
are now shredded in heaps
like paltry helpless haystacks.
A half a million are
powerless without power.
Fridges filled with stockpiled food
are now dark cabinets
starting to smell.
I knew my local grocer
would have no lines.
I dressed up
in my makeshift mask and gloves,
armed with a Clorox wipe
in my hand
and shopped.

Upon return
I spent 43 minutes
wiping and drying
my bounty.
This is a new day,
a new way that may linger
for a long time to come.
Cuomo says
"and this is a long day",
but together
we will return
to some kind of normal.
This Corona pause
will be a marker
on our collective timeline,
like pre and postwar buildings
commingled on the avenues in New York City,
that are blatant but quiet monuments
to another grand before and after.

April 15, 2020

This is kind of like
a dream come true.
I am suffering
from something that resembles
Stockholm Syndrome.
My Corona captor
has forced my children to return home
with only our 5 vessels
of flesh and bones
allowed to touch.
All other vital contact
is at a 6-foot distance,
through eyes
visible between mask edges
and furrowed brows,
or through a tempered glass screen
fogged with fingerprints and interruptions.
Meeting basic needs
is tedious but simpleminded.
I can take a walk every day
and snap pictures of the state of the world,
as I always have.
I have gained Instagram followers
during lockdown.
People are looking to belong together.
Each new number
sends a droplet of adrenaline
sidestroking through my veins.
I can walk my park path
in a clockwise direction,

going against the painted stick figures
directing traffic from the asphalt,
and see a whole new view.
Each elm tree and shadow
is fresh from behind.
I can walk smack center
up Fifth Avenue
facing limited traffic
head on,
with little threat.
In the middle of world class thoroughfares
I am momentarily invincible,
conquering ribbons of roads.
Then I return home,
scrub clean,
like my shower is a carwash
and start chopping potatoes
for another meal
together at our glass table
which is wiped clean of fingerprints
and infectious germs
at least 9 times a day.
I am so grateful
for the select-a-size paper towel
and Windex
in my arsenal,
prolonging living this basic life
with joy.

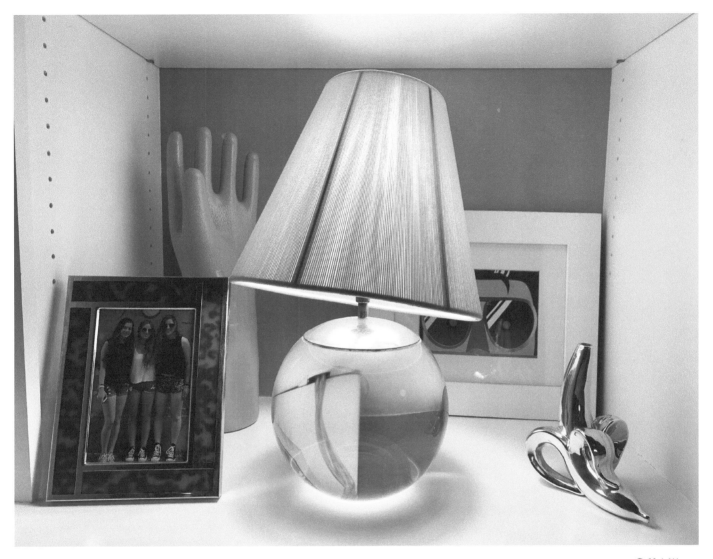

Off Kilter

Never Have I Ever

Break

You Are!!

April 18, 2020

Oh yeah,
I forgot to mention
that a few days ago
the lockdown was extended
by 2 weeks to mid-May.
No surprise.
I look back on the first few weeks
and see I was preparing for battle
mentally and inventory-wise.
Now it just is.
We are slouched and slogging along.
I am essentially acting in
the Bill Murray Groundhog Day movie,
but no one is doing my hair and makeup
or signing my paycheck.
I also pray every day
that the script won't change
as I have not memorized my lines
for when someone gets sick
and the plot twists and thickens.
I would have to improvise.

Lisa called me last night.
Her grandmother died.
Without Corona she might have made it to 101 this July,
but now she's simply done.

Her last meal was likely orange Jell-O,
never on the McDonald's menu.
She was ready and told everyone so
by refusing to talk to them.
Frankly, they are relieved.
It would have been a demotion
to live out her days
at Mary Manning Walsh,
the gateway nursing home
that was not her home.
It would have felt more cramped
than the tenement
she grew up in
where her childhood
trained her to overcome.
Lisa told me she was so poor
that she did not taste milk
until she was 16.
We grew up learning
the standard immigration unit
in social studies,
reading textbooks with pixilated photographs
of immigrant artifacts
and large, devout families
sleeping in 1 room.
Even in black and white
we saw the color of the fruits
piled high on rickety pushcarts.

A handful of these people
achieved founding father status
of great American companies.
Most did not,
but all of their apples
were a deeper red
than those from which they fled.
In another century
Covid-19 will still be embedded
in digital textbooks
and children will study
our example of disaster
and how it can lead to societal improvement.
Perhaps now,
we will know the names of our cashiers
without having to read their badges,
and teachers will be able to live off their salaries.
By the way,
Lisa's grandmother's name
was Frieda.

Just Wear It

I'll Be There For You

April 21, 2020

The shock wore off
and week 6 began.
Last week milk and eggs were being dumped,
this week it's barrels of oil.
A collective anesthesia
is seeping in.
Numbers are moving in the right direction
but we have a long way to go.
The natives are calming down
and at the same time
are restless.
I've seen lots of bad haircuts
on my screens.
Buzzed, bald and banged heads
shedding grief
into a pile of wiry hairs
that can be swept up
or dust busted
and deposited in the trash.
There was a mass shooting in Nova Scotia,
20 dead so far.
4/20 came and went.
There have been no mass shootings here,
only because we cannot gather.
The artillery is at rest.

We started a LEGO
of the Friends' Central Perk coffee house.
It's a plastic construction
of a make-believe time
when we could sit in a café
and nurse overpriced lattes.
The tables were close enough to eavesdrop
on someone else's late-night escapades
and pretend they belonged to us all.
Now, my Nespresso machine
brews all day,
as we wake at 4 different times
and need to caffeinate at different rates.
The noise from the milk frother
momentarily drowns out
the wail of the sirens
pulling up to the hospital
out my window.
I miss the roar of rush hour traffic
and the broken car alarms
set off by anything and everything.
Now the quiet and vacant streets,
are simply too loud.

April 26, 2020

I am wrestling with this mask.
It's just that much harder
to take a deep satisfying breath
with a face covering.
I can get used to
waiting on line to enter the market,
sending me in a time machine
to stand in breadlines of the Great Depression,
but this cloth gagging me
is stifling.
When I knew the mask was about to be mandated,
I tried to order some of these shields
on Amazon.
I added them to my cart
but the delivery date was closer to Memorial Day
than Saint Patrick's Day,
so, I emptied my cart.
Sandy told me to look on Etsy.
I bought 8 machine washable masks for us,
with elastic that would comfortably fit
around our ears,
while supporting an artisan sewer
in a garret somewhere.
I could throw one in the wash
after each outing
for air or pears
from the warzone.
They came fresh and pressed,
with cute, chic black and white patterns.
I used to dress well,
in clothing with zippers and buttons
that reminded me to have good posture.

Now most days,
forgiving elastic or spandex hugs my middle,
comforting me with few restrictions.
The masks are fading fast
and wrinkled all the time,
but still do the trick.
We will remain unidentifiable
at least through the summer.
I may need to find some pastel masks
for late June
when my black and white sweats
will get traded in for some color.
It is really something to see
most people walking around outside
faceless with anonymous noses and lips.
It's like I'm on the set
of some sci-fi show
filming for Hulu,
and I never enjoyed science fiction at all.
To see a little girl
in a pink piggy raincoat
with her hood up,
and its 2 little rubber ears
pointing skyward,
frolic in green frog boots
and giggle through a mask,
is simply enough to put me
over the edge.

Sheet Music

Through The Looking Glass

April 28, 2020

I do not take the bus now
because I have nowhere to go.
But some must take the bus.
I noticed the new method
to this madness.
Masked passengers board and exit
only through the rear door
and sit behind a clear curtain
and a yellow plastic chain link barrier,
positioned several feet beyond
the mortal, masked MTA driver,
keeping the virus at bay.
Transit workers have been dying
as they usher the other essential
to their posts,
shift after shift.
Homeless folks are camped out
in the subways.
I am not sure where they go to the bathroom.
New problems pile up
on top of old issues
like strains of this pandemic
that vary so greatly
from asymptomatic to suicidal.
Dr. Laura Breen
survived Covid
and went back to work at her hospital
but died right after
by suicide.
Feeding our healthcare workers
free lunch is just not enough.

I want to get on the subway.
I long to ride the rails,
to journey beyond my neighborhood
and explore other urban textures.
The L train work is now complete.
It is finished 3 months ahead of schedule
because there were so few riders
impeding progress.
When will the dancers and surfers return?
I grew up avoiding the graffiti encrusted subway
and its tracks of felonious trouble
and lesser crimes.
For how long will I be afraid once again
to descend below ground,
swipe my MetroCard
and expose myself to billions of microorganisms?
Germs were always present
but before they would likely only affect me.
Now, once I reach my destination
and rise above ground,
I can easily harm
anyone standing next to me.

April 29, 2020

Today I am one of the stages of grief.
Today I am angry.
I walk fast and hard
early this morning in a drizzle
as I have a busy day on Zoom.
At noon I have my first virtual shiva.
I would like to do my hair for it.
Peter's father died.
He was loved,
88
and did not have Covid.
He had one of the bad cancers.
Peter knew he would die
and for years prepared himself,
likely for a magical goodbye moment,
a funeral on the Upper West Side
filled with rows of support
and a eulogy about legacy.
Peter is a writer.
It would have been a doozy.
Hundreds of people
were expected to roll through
his parents' Fifth Avenue classic 8,
well lit,
well lived in apartment,
for a full week.
Instead, when Papa took the turn,
Peter and his brother decided
to drive and drive
out of isolation in Windham
to Florida.

They missed his last breath
by about an hour.
Peter had much less time
to prepare himself for
this extraordinary new breed of mourning.
He sits in Miami with Mama
for the week.
His wife and children
are locked down apart
from their link
to their beloved father-in-law and grandfather.
I hope people are sending casseroles.
Today at noon
my oldest friends and I
will gather around Peter's screen
and sit together
to talk about Papa.
We all need intimacy and rugelach.
I am a bit nervous about dialing in
just as I might be before
traversing the threshold
of any shiva house.
These jitters
are the most normal thing I have felt
in the past 6 weeks.
For that I am grateful.

Sign Of Hope

Open For Business

Thank You Health Heroes

Top Of The Morning To You

May 1, 2020

April just evaporated
and now it's May 1st.
Mayday, mayday
I cry for help,
as does everyone else around the world,
drowning each other out.
A big business trip for me
is cancelled.
I was willing to take
an 8-seater prop plane
which was not optimal
when booked,
but now would be ideal.
I felt like a daredevil
when I agreed to take the tiny flight.
Today my adrenaline rushes
each time I risk my life
and go to the grocery
or reclaim my favorite walking path
which is too narrow
for social distance.
I conquer these little battles daily,
or maybe I don't.
Perhaps in 2 weeks
I will get sick from exercising
or buying a lemon.

My work as an interior designer
is evaporating too.
I spent 2 decades
making people's homes beautiful
enough to reflect their souls and their goals
and be the perfect landing pad
for the precious little time
they had at home.
Little did I know
I was setting up
bomb shelters
for when a global pandemic
blew lethal particles
of destruction
into our air clouds
and onto our Amazon packages.
With a decomposing economy
who will want to replace their carpet
because they are finally tired
of the color gray?
Who will want to demolish walls
while we build the world back up?
We stay home.
The middle spot on my velvet sofa
bends and gives a bit more every day,
adjusting to its extended burden.
I have chipped most of my everyday plates and bowls.

I am wearing out my house,
and tearing through my sweats,
while my tailored wardrobe
goes out of style,
just hanging there,
in my dark dusty closet.
I cannot imagine
how it will feel
to wear a shoe all day.
But when I can
I will put on my most crisp jeans,
ones without trendy holes
manufactured into the knees,
and a plain white tee,
and venture out
with my longer, grayer hair,
into the new world,
forever changed by air.

School Shoes

Lunch Is Served

May 4, 2020

The Javits Center
has emptied out,
its hospital beds and respirators
will no longer need to convene there.
The SS Comfort
has been hosed down
and has sailed off
into the Hudson River sunset,
leaving a gaping hole
on the pier
like a missing tooth.
The pop-up field hospital
in my park
has admitted its last patient
and will slowly fold into itself and disappear.

I have had my windows open
more than I usually do,
forcing fresh air
down our throats and into our lungs,
while a film of black soot
slowly settles on our sills.
I have let in a few flies.
They say it's safe to open our windows
and I do,
but is it different when we live
directly across from a hospital?

I am afraid to enter Pick-A-Bagel
on my corner.
I applaud that every Monday
they feed the hospital workers
for free,
but it is a small and narrow store
and I am scared of their extra-large,
baked on the premises,
everything bagels.
Often they were still warm from the oven
and the fresh baked smell
would escape the brown paper bag
and waft subtly through my kitchen.
So many people are baking bread.
I am not one of them.
I do not have the patience
for yeast to rise.
I really miss their tuna too.
I did not stock up
on red, white and blue tin cans
of Bumble Bee solid white albacore.
I grew up eating that tuna
all the time.
That stout can is a remembrance of my youth.
I have not bought even 1 in years
because I have come to rely on Pick-A-Bagel's
thin plastic pint
populating my fridge.

I saw birdwatchers in the park yesterday.
They stood apart
and together aimed their binoculars skyward
at warblers in a big tall tree.
I could not see them
with my naked eyes
above my favorite gray mask
with white stars.
The grass is so green now.
The tulips are extra bulbous
and the many varieties of pink and yellow park flowers
are deeper in color than usual.
Even the urban earth
can catch its breath
while we stay home
and our cars remain idle.
This magnificent intensity
ushers in week 8.
The numbers are all dropping
and I will patiently wait
for instructions on reopening,
and then see how quickly
that will tone down
the prettiest cherry blossoms
I have ever seen.

We Can Still Smell The Flowers Through Our Masks

Renewal

May 5, 2020

I saw something purple
in the grass.
I thought it was a fallen hydrangea
but then saw it was a surgical glove.
Now there are steep fines
for littering used masks and gloves.
A man in a parks department provided surgical mask
is mowing the lawn
adjacent to the field hospital.
Another is weed whacking.
The sounds from their machinery
hum together melodically.
The grass keeps growing.
They cut for the symphony
and the maintenance of hope.
The scent of renewal
breaks through the fabric filter
over my face
and no one can see my smile.

May 7, 2020

Reopening is going to be like purgatory.
We will be waiting to see
what happens next.
Constant counting
and never ending numbers
have been thrown at us for months.
Can people exhale and get haircuts
without fueling the next wave?
Will the back of children's thighs
feel the burn
of overheated playground slides?
New Yorkers need their hot dog carts
and salty street pretzels.
I do not eat them often
but I like knowing they are there,
trademarking my cement sidewalks
in the same way they did
when I was a child.
Several food cart vendors
abandoned their carts
in front of the Metropolitan Museum of Art.

They left them near the curb,
facing the grand entrance
and saluting
the granite steps.
One rusting cart says
"tow please" in permanent marker.
Another is still filled with plastic Coke bottles
and Poland Spring waters.
A veteran vendor
left his Naugahyde swivel chair too.
I have yet to see anyone
sit in the seat
and drink the sodas
while spinning round and round.

Disabled Veteran From Another War

Wear A Mask

Bus Station

May 8, 2020

I was in my first Spike Lee movie last night.
I was wearing sweats.
At the end of another CNN
Anderson Cooper and Sanjay Gupta town hall,
they welcomed Spike
and rolled his 3-minute short
valentine to New York.
He covered unpopulated scenes
in the 5 boroughs,
with their emptiness echoing
through the canyons, parks and bridges
that interconnect us.
Near the end
heroic, hopeful doctors and nurses
start to appear at a 7pm
clap because we care moment.
And then boom,
there we were,
the 5 of us like the boroughs,
squeezed together,
cheering and screaming
from our cramped balcony.

Of course all of this
is set to Sinatra's anthem
New York, New York.
We appear as he belts the line
"if I can make it there, I'll make it anywhere".
I'd like to think that New York raised me.
I even have a dark gray and white graphic tee shirt
that says so.
I need to get 3 more shirts
for my 3 boroughs
who have been forced
to grow upward and outward
over the last 2 months
living at home
in the eye of the storm.

Off Limits

Thank You

May 12 ,2020

This morning I was brave enough
to walk directly by
the field hospital in Central Park.
I have been staying away
from Mount Sinai Hospital
which is odd
since I cannot avoid Lenox Hill Hospital,
right outside my window.
The last white tent was coming down.
It looks like I imagine Coachella looks
when it's packing up.
Con Ed was there disconnecting
and Samaritan's Purse trucks
and Jesus Christ
lined Fifth Avenue,
collecting the contaminated parts.
I saw a small but life size
plaster of paris sculpture
of a boy in a Spiderman eye mask
and a yellow cape.
His hard, hollow body is seated
on a splintery park bench
right outside the field.
He wears powerful red boots
painted on his little legs,
and of course, a real surgical mask
and matching gloves
with which he holds a sign
that says thank you.

It is clearly written in rainbow markers
by someone who has not been
writing for too long.
The placard alongside
says this project was
a father son collaboration,
and beautiful, boneless figurines like this
are being placed outside of hospitals
and essential businesses
to say thank you.
I can picture the look-alike pair
in their kitchen
surrounded by heaps of cloth and wire
to be cut and glued into pasty flesh
and skeletal structures.
There was probably red paint
that dripped onto their tile
and permanently stained their grout.
This little handmade boy
propped up on an old bench,
screams love and appreciation
louder than all the respirators
that were in the park,
and all the traffic that once raced
and will soon flow again
down Fifth Avenue.

May 15, 2020

How the hell is it Friday,
sheet day, Friyay,
76 days since the first case in New York?
This week went quickly,
likely because the weather is good.
Lockdown will lift
in 5 regions upstate today.
They will manufacture
and construct again.
I will wash my white sheets.
I must remember to remove
my new red mask from the machine,
as it will surely run
and leave me with pink tinted bedding.

Almost every Friday for the last 2 ½ years
Susie and I have quit work early
and walked while window shopping,
then settled around my kitchen table
for some wine.
Our ritual includes
cashew nuts, rippled chips
and very special wine glasses
that are like small crystal fishbowls,
balanced on delicate stems.
I have broken and replaced several.
I only have 2 left
and use them solely
for this special occasion.

The last time we met in person
I was a little afraid to be sharing
finger food from small bowls,
but I did
and we did not get sick.
Will we ever intermix our fingers in a snack dish again?
When Covid contained us,
we began to Friyay over FaceTime
and invited Pam and Ronnie
to join us.
When we resume seeing people again,
perhaps they will still dial in.
Somehow Fridays do still feel like Fridays,
and the weekends still feel like weekends.

I am dreading more laundry
and this load comes with folding
a king size sheet set
relatively neatly
and making a king size bed.
Discussing domesticity over Zoom,
Amy taught me
it's much more effective
to put a fitted sheet on
wrapping its elastic edges
in a diagonal order.
That's the trick.
Bottom right, then top left…
Going forward,
every time I change sheets,
I will be reminded of Covid.

Rainbow After The Rain

I ♥ NY More Than Ever

I got 5 new masks
in the mail today.
They came from Turkey.
They actually arrived yesterday
but we leave packages untouched
for 24 hours now.
The seamstress packs them
beautifully in individual Ziplocks
and then into a mylar decorative pouch
that looks like
it's for sanitary napkin disposal.
I sense the humanity of the craftsman
as I unwrap.
There is a plain white one
that instantly reminded me
of my grandfather's handkerchiefs.
After a few washes it will resemble
the crumpled tissues
I find in my pockets,
but for a little while,
I think of Pa.

Our lockdown is officially extended
for another month
which is a little longer
than I expected,
and those few extra days
hit me hard.
Maybe soon
Susie and I will be able to walk
6 feet apart
up Madison Avenue,
and peer into the empty stores,
at least the ones
that are not boarded up
with plywood.
Then we can sit outside,
pull down our masks
and swig wine
from Swell water bottles,
while we FaceTime Pam and Ronnie
for Friyay.

May 16, 2020

I just realized
I can wear white again next week.
Memorial Day will come and go.
Best laid plans, cancelled,
but on Monday I can wear
my summer uniform white jeans.
For weeks now
I've been meaning to
clean out my closet
and move my heavy sweaters up high,
where my shorts hibernate for the winter.
Early on in the pandemic
I kept busy cleaning out our cabinets
and drawers.
When I tackled the kitchen
I found I had 2 metal lids
that no longer had pots.
They became cymbals
for our 7 o'clock orchestra of applause.
I leave them on my dining room floor
by my slip-on sneakers at the balcony door.
Sometimes the late afternoon sun
hits them just so,
and the glint is beautifully blinding.
I have lost my organizational momentum
and I can't reach my summer clothes.

When I eventually
muster up the might
to change over my closet,
I will not take down any Saturday night special
wedged espadrilles,
or summer bags
made of straw.
I have not carried a purse in months.
Sunglasses are tricky.
They fog up because of the mask.
I have not worn any jewelry
other than my plain gold wedding band
that matches Doug's.
In fact,
I have not been outside after dark
at all.
My neighborhood is desolate at night,
except for the ambulances
that still arrive and depart,
and a single yellow taxi
that waits at the corner of the hospital
several nights a week.
I imagine it's a nurse's partner
retrieving a loved one
from another day at war.

Waiting For 7pm

'Tis The Season

May 17, 2020

I just decided
if I die in the summer
I would like a Mister Softee truck
outside my funeral.
I'd like to give everyone a free cone
to catch their tears,
and drown any sorrows
in the sweet simple melody
the trucks blare
to take us back to simpler times.
I will remain loyal
after I'm gone.
It will have to be an authentic
red, white and royal blue
Mister Softee,
not one of the many
imposters or copy cats
with their tempting colorful trucks.

Yesterday, Lexie and I
had our first soft serve
of the season.
We both had chocolate sprinkles.
This is not the first spring
we have done this together,
so you could call it a tradition.
My vanilla chocolate swirl
never looked so beautiful.
To remove my mask
for 4 minutes
to battle to consume it
before all the sprinkles
dripped onto my hands,
was a delightful challenge.
I thought about the risk
of eating street food
during a pandemic
and decided not to resist.
There were signs posted
on the side of the truck
reminding customers to social distance
and Mister Softee himself
wore a distinguished mask
with an ice cream patch sewn on.
Stealing this brief moment of normalcy
tasted so damn good.

Nothing Will Stop Us

It's A Sign

Bright New Day

May 21, 2020

The city sidewalks
will be stained
for a while,
with markings painted on
or taped down
in front of stores
so we know how and where
to wait to gain entry.
Strokes of orange in front of Citarella,
dashes of the green
between kelly and forest
leading to Starbucks pickup,
and blue at FedEx,
all measured neatly
at roughly 6 feet apart.
These pictorial instructions
are like hieroglyphics
carved deeply and carefully
into cave walls
recounting the times.
The interior store floors
are marked too,
and that duct tape
doesn't stick for long
with all the foot traffic
and shopping cart wheels
catching the gooey edges.

Memorial Day Weekend is coming
and I still haven't touched my closet.
I see people loading up their cars
for long weekend getaways,

kicking off the summer
like it's summer.
I am still here,
sticking to the pavement.
I am itching to go on an outing
to a beach or a field
where I still would not escape
the tape and the paint,
as many are controlling social distance in nature,
with linear demarcations.
I predict that one of the most iconic images
of our city during Corona,
will be the newly gentrified
Domino Park in Williamsburg, Brooklyn,
with its painted white rings
laid out on the green grass,
to contain people
in their own one-dimensional orbits.
This will appear in the digital textbooks.
I dream often
of impossible travel.
I am in a subway or train station
darting from gate to gate
but getting nowhere.
People's dreams are different for now.
I'd like to fall asleep one night
and dream I am climbing high
on an unmarked mountain,
rising step by step toward the top,
without sticky tape residue
on the bottom of my shoe,
holding me back.

May 25, 2020

As a nation we fly our flags,
still barbeque
and celebrate Memorial Day today,
as we approach
100,000 dead from Covid.
The New York death toll was under 100
but rose back up yesterday.
The New York Times published
a black and white cover
that will live in infamy,
listing the names, locations
and a small detail
of 1000 Americans
who have succumbed.
"Master of jazz guitar, fire chief who answered the call on 9/11,
Seahawks season ticket holder, retired meter-reader
and proud mother of three."
This is the new 1%.
The refrigerated truck on my street,
from Grand Forks, North Dakota
is gone.
One to go.

I have a long history
with Lenox Hill Hospital.
Even as I moved around
it has always been
in my neighborhood.
In elementary school either Joanne or Sarah,
one of the identical twins in my class,
had her appendix taken out there.

My first memory of the hospital
was having fun at her bedside
while visiting with my friends.
It was a guilty pleasure
to have such a good time at a hospital.

My OB practices there
and that is where all 3 of my children were delivered.
By the time Valerie was born,
we lived across the street.
48 hours after her arrival
we wrapped her tightly
in the same pale yellow velour onesie
her sisters wore,
expertly swaddled her
in a Lenox Hill issued cotton baby blanket,
and gently placed her in our old carriage.
She ventured out into the world
through the back entrance
like a celebrity,
and drew her first breath
of New York street air
right where the tents are now.
We wheeled her 25 yards
and were home.

When my mother was sick
she did a few tours of duty
at Lenox Hill.
It was where she spent her last overnight on earth
and was lucky enough to make it home to die
on her own wool carpeted floor.

You Clap For Us, We Kneel For You

Color Is Not A Crime

During the final 3 years
of my father's battle,
he essentially lived at Lenox Hill.
From some of his rooms
I was even able to look into
my own living room.
I remember seeing my downstairs neighbor's
fat Christmas tree.
On a Thursday he was on hospice
and that Sunday he died there,
in a sunny sterile corner room.
I pass that window almost daily
count up to the 4th floor,
and am reminded.

Statistically, my parents
should still be here.
Statistically, they would have been
at high risk for Corona.
I am tickled they missed this.

Each morning for the last 20 years
I open my bedroom shades
and the hospital
is the first thing I see.

Last fall Lenox Hill announced
a grand expansion project
with a 10 year, 3 phase construction plan,
and the tallest towers in my zip code,
that would defy zoning laws
and darken the city,

casting a trendy charcoal shadow
on Central Park's green.
Local buildings and businesses
banded together to fight the hospital.
Community board meetings
in dated orange auditoriums
were finally crowded.
I was angry
every time I walked by the hospital buildings.
I felt trapped,
unable to sell my apartment for years.
Now I am trapped and angry
for very different reasons.
Though as I process the noble impact of Covid,
all of my fury
drains from my veins.
I instantly see the physical presence
of gleaming limestone
and mostly brick
that contains Lenox Hill Hospital,
as a fortress of goodness
housing royal human heroes.
My pride and gratitude
for my hospital
connects me to the world over
and soothes me,
for the lifelong history above.

A Day At The Beach

May 28, 2020

I ventured out this morning
to find the last refrigerated truck
is gone.
I wept a bit
beneath my mask.
I decided to walk north,
up to Harlem today.
I crave a break from seeking
Covid photos to take.
The abundance of hand colored rainbows and hearts,
and the general population
hiding the majority of their expressions
behind their masks,
had become my obsession.
I needed to find
the regular urban texture
that defines big cities for me.
I have made a conscious decision
to adjust my mindset
to embrace this temporary new normal.
This is what summer 2020
will look like.
My mask will constantly be damp
from perspiration and breath.
I will stop wearing sweats.
I need to make the most of it.

My explorations are constrained
to where my legs can carry me
and carry me back,
and also, to the elasticity
of my bladder.
My last adventure before lockdown
was to Coney Island.
Lexie and I took the Q train
to Stillwell Avenue,
the very last stop.
It was an exceptionally sunny
and warm day in March.
Lexie had never been.
We walked on Surf Avenue
in the footsteps of Mermaid Parades past,
into the giant Nathan's Famous
and an old school candy store,
with red, white and blue paneled walls,
penny candy and hard ice cream.
We chatted with the generational owner.
His soft serve machine
would be turned on soon.
We peered into Luna Park
at the gleaming, colorful rides.
Workers were setting up,
test running roller coasters,
preparing to launch them
in a matter of weeks.

The signs on the fences
declared opening day on April 4th.
This was the 100th anniversary
of the Wonder Wheel!
That's a lot of rotations
and momentum to stop.
It would take a pandemic
to halt the rides
and keep them from demonstrating physics
to New York youth.
I took my shoes off
and we walked on the beach.
At least my bare feet
could meld with the sand
once this year.
I found a crushed blue
Corona Extra beer bottlecap
on the shore
and took a picture of it
with the iconic red steeple parachute jump
in the background.
I thought it was a funny photo,
an ironic statement.
I took the flattened cap home with me
and put it away
in a keepsake box.
Little did I know the magnitude
of what would happen next.

Today I did see
the dilapidated storefronts
I like to photograph.
I observed how cracking paint
reflects the flat white light
of a cloudy day.
I passed small churches
and a simple funeral home
that looked like a movie set,
but I know there is an actual chapel
beyond the front.
The sidewalk had room
for the big, black hearse
to park on the curb and kiss the building.
I saw mourners dressed up
and comforting one another.
In that moment
it did not matter if the dead
died from Covid
or some other cause.
The grief is all the same.

Jump In

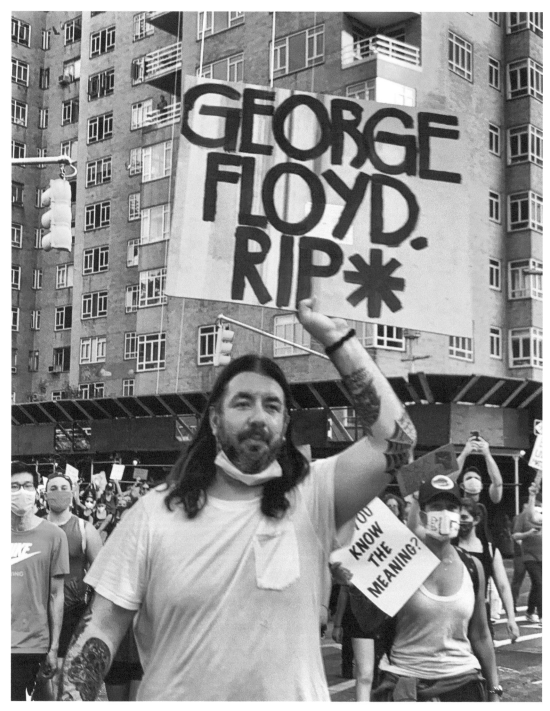

Rest In Power

May 30, 2020

This is the verse
I did not want to write.
This is the plot twist
I did not see coming now,
but it has been coming for centuries.
George Floyd
was murdered in Minneapolis
at the white knee
of some brutal police.
There is no way
to make sense
of the video
we were all still home to watch over and over
on repeat on our scratched
and cracked screens.
This is the news story
that finally outran Corona.
This is the novel festering nightmare.
The nation is setting itself on futile fire
in protest.
As we actually approach reopening
and Cuomo has deemed it
NY Forward,
I had started to think about my last entry
to this chronicle.
I planned to end it
with the positivity
of all that was created
out of the world
that was locked down,
together apart,
bound by hateful air

that would rest
and bring permanent renewal.
The world was to be a different place after,
much of the change
for my children's future good,
but it is no different than before.
The long rest culminates in unrest
and 40 million jobless Americans.
We have taken 2 steps backwards.
America is spiraling from grace.
Black and brown
beaten down by Corona
is the same story
as the crushing,
strangling,
infinite shots fired,
knee on the neck
attack
that is another plague
for which only the few
seek a vaccine.
For the first time in 11 weeks,
I feel sick.

Can You Imagine?

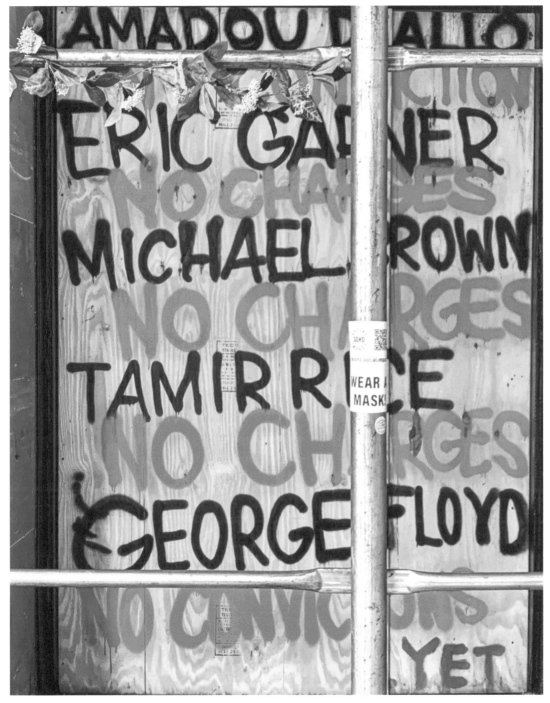

No Charges

June 2, 2020

Today is #blackouttuesday.
My social media feeds are bright
with deep black squares
showing solidarity as I scroll,
and shining a light
on the Black Lives Matter movement.
The stores are boarded up
but that doesn't necessarily
swear off violent intruders.
The grain of plywood
always fascinates me.
I love to photograph its contrasts.
It is a sketchbook of a forest's x-ray,
morphed into other objects.
Now it will be that visual
I can never unsee,
offering merely a thin layer of protection,
only days before reopening.

After dark across the nation
evil prevails.
Broken glass, firecrackers
and empty black and blue Adidas boxes
litter the sidewalks
leaving trails of tear gas,
rubber bullets
and riotous anarchy
in their wake.
After 80 years of being deemed
the city that never sleeps,
New York has a curfew.
My overnight doorman Wagner
was nervous.

We offered him a cup of tea.
But at dawn
the neighbors come out
with brooms from their closets
and sweep up the shattered glass.
In the light of day
peaceful protesters pound the pavement.
Police take a knee,
while hand in hand
with marchers.
19 block long crowds
cover the streets.
As the passionate wave of the protest voices
bounced off our window,
we ran out and joined
the mile-long crowd
of hope and cosmic change.
"No justice no peace."
Screaming "don't shoot"
for 60 seconds
could not possibly make me understand,
but I ached
as I formed the words
with my lips and lungs
from beneath my mask.
As I chanted
I felt safe from the virus
with masked marchers
keeping their Corona breath
at a distance.
The health crisis fueled our cries,
planted seeds of power,
not stifling us at all.

Batten Down The Hatches

Blank Slate

June 3, 2020

All of the avenues
have become a sea of plywood storefronts.
In 2 days
I have adapted
and the visual sting
of my wooden city
has worn off.
On TV I have seen looters
tear through it
with sheer rage
and the might of their bare hands.
Saks Fifth Avenue, directly across from Rockefeller Center
and next to Saint Patrick's Cathedral,
has added barbed wire,
flood lights, and guards stationed
every 6 feet
from 49th to 50th Street,
another sight I will never unsee.
Window shopping has gone dark for now.

I am exploring the aftermath
in Flatiron and Union Square.
I see @thechalkjungle
pastel scribblings of hope
on the fresh, thin grainy wood.
I see painters rolling
building colored paint
over last night's barely dry graffiti.
The greenmarket is in full swing,
like a normal Wednesday morning.
Nothing will keep our New York asleep.
Snow White was just a fairy tale.
These sidewalk chalk cartoon hearts
are real.
New York Tough
is a gene that cannot be altered.

June 6, 2020

We have had 4 relatively calm nights
with no major looting
but a lot of arrested protesters
who have violated the 8:00 curfew.
With new bail reform laws,
it's much less of an event.
The early June weather
is hot and humid,
reminding me of Spike Lee's
Do the Right Thing.
30 years later
I still see the sexless sex scene
when Mookie slides ice cubes
over Tina's bare skin.
It's the image I remember most
from that early film
on the hottest day of summer,
battling and settling the heat.

Every time I pull my mask down
to take a truly deep enough breath,
I hear the words
I can't breathe.
I see a perfectly formed dandelion
and instinctively want to pick it
and decimate the seed head
to make a wish
like I did when I was 6 years old.
I don't,
because blowing extra breath
could endanger my neighbors.
I shrug it off
since we cannot wish away
all of this chaos anyway.

Let This Be A Peaceful Day In Our Nation

Patience And Fortitude

June 8, 2020

New York City is open,
coincidentally on the 100th day
since the first case here.
Phase 1 has begun.
I am excited for the first time
since that week
when I thought the death toll would peak.
Free masks and New York State Clean
hand sanitizer are being handed out
atop the subway stairs.
I took a bottle
as a limited-edition souvenir
of this very strange time in my life.
I positioned it on display
on my bookcase.
The fountains outside
the shuttered Met Museum
have been turned back on.
Once more they spray
as they sing and dance
over the black stone basins
now shining and reflecting
the flags at full mast again.

June 13, 2020

I walked out of my house yesterday
for some fresh afternoon air
and intersected a peaceful protest
that I joined.
We marched forward
to Gracie Mansion,
and I snapped picture after picture
as I chanted through a mask.
There on the pavement of East End Avenue,
I took a knee in the sea of the bent,
leaning through my white jeans
into the filthy cement.
There has been actual abrupt reform,
re-funding and revolution
in less than 3 weeks
since the Memorial Day massacre
of George Floyd
was filmed on a phone.
Confederate flags have been
removed from racetracks,
statues have been defiled and toppled to the ground.
Band-Aid colors have been noted.

Today we will rent a car
that has been medical grade disinfected,
and drive south to Philadelphia
to empty out Valerie's dorm room
and to fill Julia's senior year house,
as we drop her off for the summer.
She will work remotely
confined with friends,
trying to figure out the new normal
of her generation.
Closure and beginning collide.
After 3 months together alone
huddled in our familial nest,
we will be separated
as we all try to get back
to the new and eventually improved
free world.
This summer heat should melt away
the torrid spring
and begin to pave the path to redemption
that includes new crayon colors
and consequences for all.
After more than 14 days of protests,
the Covid cases have not risen.
This is my sign
that eventually everything is
going to be alright.

We Must Do It

Don't Rain On My Parade

June 14, 2020

Poem, I put you down.
It is time to deal with the regular world again.
Thank you for steering me
through the tumultuous season
that forever transformed
my family and me,
and preparing me
to live with pride
in challenge and change.

Corona was my early muse.
Black Lives Matter has boldly taken over.
Out of these collective horrors
creativity has exploded around me
and did not spread any germs.
Days and months on pause
gestated and birthed countless
videos
memes
TikToks
baked goods
signs
chalk drawings
collaborations
essays
songs
art
photos
poetry
and verse.

Then the murder of George Floyd
brought the boiling point quarantined
out onto the streets
to react to centuries of lockdown.
Wooden boards of flimsy plywood
were erected over glass storefronts,
both before and after
extensive destruction,
and still became fresh blank canvases
for more loud, explosive
and deeply layered expression.
Some of the graffiti is beautiful,
painterly and meaningful,
while other is swift and angry,
colored with hatred
by fingers pressing as hard as humanly possible
on the delicate little spray paint buttons.
Words and mantras bleed
from the lampposts and building cornices.
Volume has been given
to the voiceless.
Our city streets look and sound
completely different
than they did just recently,
when pristine Christmas displays
waited for snow cover
that did not fall this year.

The tune of the holiday carol
has been replaced
by helicopters that circle and circle
above us
and pockets of people chanting in unison.

After arks and floods
and fire and brimstone,
renewal and purpose must rise
from the ashes and urban grit,
and in due time
the newest normal
will have to be a better normal.
It is time to stop the long pause,
hit the play button,
and inhale deeply,
so that everyone can breathe equally
at last.

Elevated

Simple Instructions

Acknowledgement

I would like to acknowledge all of those lost too soon and unnecessarily to the Covid-19 pandemic and to the ongoing struggle for equality.

I would also like to thank my community of cherished friends who bring endless love and support to my life.

Finally, I am forever grateful to my beloved husband and partner Doug and my adored daughters, Lexie, Julia and Valerie, who give humor and meaning to my days, before, during and after lockdown. Let's keep laughing!

Biography

NICOLE FREEZER RUBENS is a native New Yorker who with her husband raised their three daughters there as well. She studied studio art, art history, creative writing and photography, and following a career in the art world, launched her own boutique interior design firm.

Since she was a kid, Nicole always wrote poetry and took photos. Her favorite pastime now is exploring new neighborhoods and posting her treasured finds on Instagram. She is absolutely thrilled to combine two of her lifelong passions in her first book. Please follow Nicole on Instagram @nfrconsult.

CPSIA information can be obtained
at www.ICGtesting.com
Printed in the USA
LVHW072006041220
673096LV00026B/565